Published by:

KOLORA kato

This book belongs to:

....

PLAY WITH YOUR IMAGINATION

PLAY WITH YOUR IMAGINATION

PLAY WITH YOUR IMAGINATION

PLAY WITH YOUR IMAGINATION

PLAY WITH YOUR IMAGINATION

PLAY WITH YOUR IMAGINATION

PLAY WITH YOUR IMAGINATION

PLAY WITH YOUR IMAGINATION

PLAY WITH YOUR IMAGINATION

PLAY WITH YOUR IMAGINATION

PLAY WITH YOUR IMAGINATION

PLAY WITH YOUR IMAGINATION

PLAY WITH YOUR IMAGINATION

PLAY WITH YOUR IMAGINATION

PLAY WITH YOUR IMAGINATION

PLAY WITH YOUR IMAGINATION

PLAY WITH YOUR IMAGINATION

PLAY WITH YOUR IMAGINATION

PLAY WITH YOUR IMAGINATION

PLAY WITH YOUR IMAGINATION

PLAY WITH YOUR IMAGINATION

PLAY WITH YOUR IMAGINATION

PLAY WITH YOUR IMAGINATION

PLAY WITH YOUR IMAGINATION

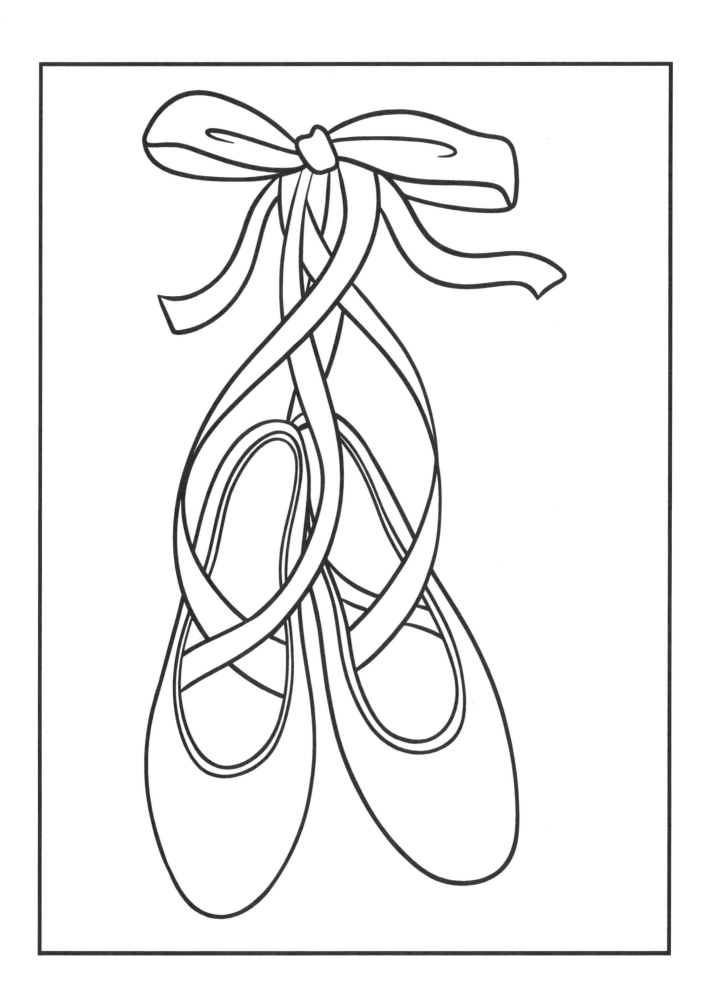

PLAY WITH YOUR IMAGINATION

PLAY WITH YOUR IMAGINATION

PLAY WITH YOUR IMAGINATION

PLAY WITH YOUR IMAGINATION

PLAY WITH YOUR IMAGINATION

PLAY WITH YOUR IMAGINATION

PLAY WITH YOUR IMAGINATION

PLAY WITH YOUR IMAGINATION

PLAY WITH YOUR IMAGINATION

PLAY WITH YOUR IMAGINATION

PLAY WITH YOUR IMAGINATION

PLAY WITH YOUR IMAGINATION

PLAY WITH YOUR IMAGINATION

PLAY WITH YOUR IMAGINATION

PLAY WITH YOUR IMAGINATION

PLAY WITH YOUR IMAGINATION

PLAY WITH YOUR IMAGINATION

KOLORA kato

Thank you for purchasing this coloring book!

I hope you enjoy hours of creativity and fun immersed in its pages.

Your support means a lot and encourages me to continue creating and sharing creative and quality content for the youngest members of the family.

So, I'd like to ask you a little favor:

Could you consider leaving a **review**?
Posting a review is the best and easiest way to support independent authors like me. It would mean a lot to me.

Made in United States
Troutdale, OR
11/30/2024

25535495R00051